GW00891002

Sing, Clap and Play the Recorder Book 1

A descant recorder book
for beginners
Heather Cox and Garth Rickard
Designed and illustrated by David Woodroffe

Nelson

To the teacher

For many years school music has been considered a 'special' subject, demanding a rare and particular talent. Consequently, teachers have shied away from it, leaving their pupils either with no music, or at best waiting for the once-a-week lesson with the specialist.

This book is written specifically to enable the teacher with little or no musical background to teach the recorder. Specialist teachers may also find it a useful backbone for their courses. The book is aimed at children of 7 to 9 years.

The lessons should take about two terms to complete. Three concerts are included, and much of the 'SING, CLAP and PLAY' material could also be performed, thus making a concert not so much a special occasion, but more a way of life. Each lesson should take between one and two weeks. We suggest one half-hour session per week, and five minutes every day for practice.
The importance of short, daily practices cannot be stressed enough.

The learning of any musical instrument demands continual attention to detail and accuracy. Throughout the book 'special hints' for teachers are printed in boxes.
These are of a practical nature.

The sequence 'SING, CLAP and PLAY' is fundamental to the book. Singing and clapping helps the child to establish the rhythm through the words, and in time he will begin to associate a pitch with a written note.

Introduction

This is your recorder.

Hold it between the fingers and thumb
of your **left** hand.

Support it with the thumb
of your **right** hand.

Until you are ready to play,
rest the mouthpiece on your chin.[1]

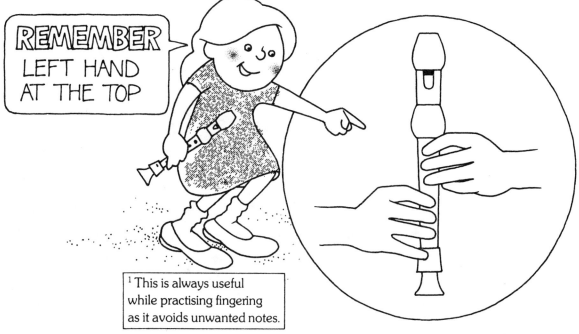

REMEMBER LEFT HAND AT THE TOP

[1] This is always useful
while practising fingering
as it avoids unwanted notes.

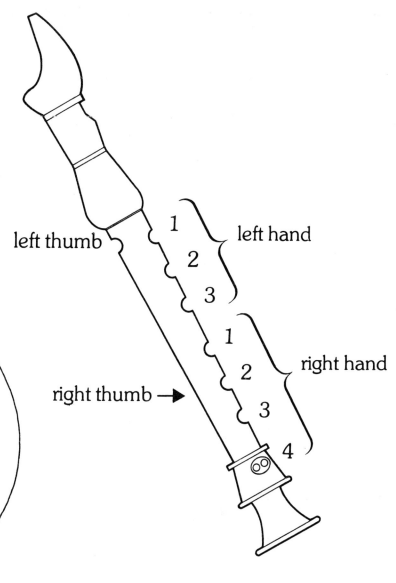

left thumb

left hand
1
2
3

right thumb →

right hand
1
2
3
4

Lesson 1

left hand
1
left thumb

To play the note *B*, lift up all your fingers, except the first finger of your left hand and your left thumb.[1]

B

Place your lips over the mouthpiece and make your tongue say 'doo' into the recorder.[2]

Try this several times, blowing softly and making all the notes sound the same.[3]

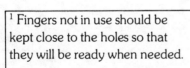

DOO   DOO   DOO

DOO

[1] Fingers not in use should be kept close to the holes so that they will be ready when needed.

[2] Every note at this stage should be tongued to give a clear beginning.

[3] For a well-pitched note, blowing softly is essential.

Sing, Clap and Play 1

Here is your first song.

1 Sing it.

2 Clap it.

3 Play it.[1]

Practise this several times, and then go on to the other songs.

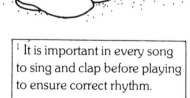

BOOTS!

Count –[2]
1-2-3-4-

Brown boots, black boots,   left,   right,   left,   right!

BACH

Count –
1-2-3-4

Bach played bag-pipes   in   a brass band —.

[1] It is important in every song to sing and clap before playing to ensure correct rhythm.

[2] A slow, steady count will indicate the speed of the song, and will start everyone together.

BIG, BAD BILL

Count –
1 - 2 - 3 - 4

Bill was a ban-dit, big, bad and bold —, Burst in the Bank and pinched all the gold.

5

Lesson 2

The note A is played with the
first two fingers and thumb
of your *left* hand.[1]

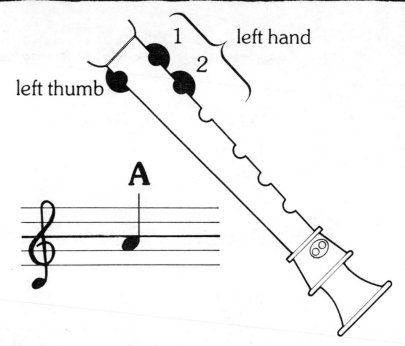

Keep your other fingers close to the holes.

Practise A several times, and then
go on to SING, CLAP and PLAY.

DOO

REMEMBER
'DOO' INTO THE
RECORDER

BLOW SOFTLY

[1] Using the pads of the fingers
ensures a good 'seal' and
avoids squeaking.

Sing, Clap and Play 2

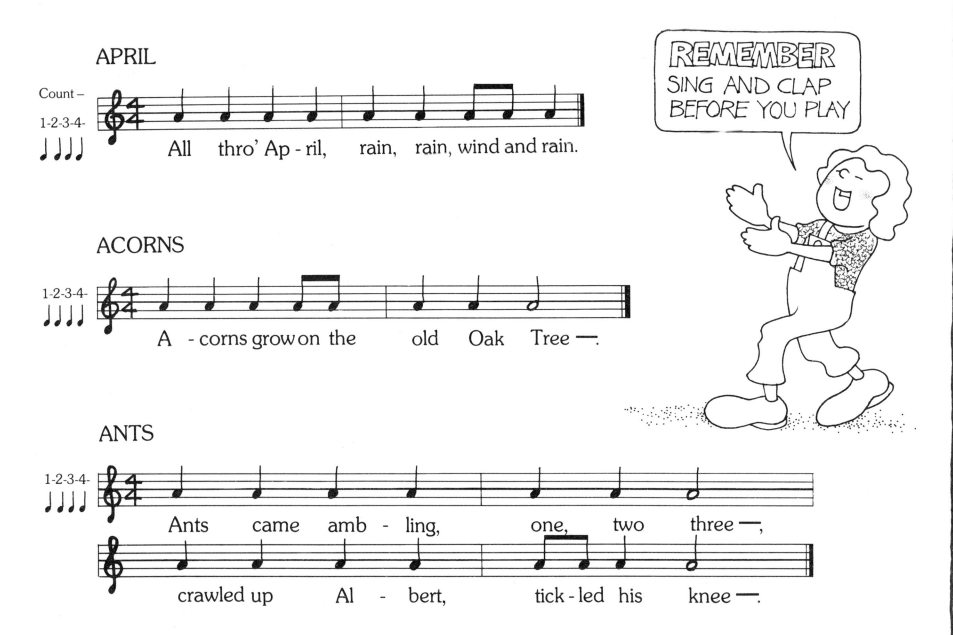

APRIL

Count –
1-2-3-4-

All thro' Ap - ril, rain, rain, wind and rain.

REMEMBER
SING AND CLAP
BEFORE YOU PLAY

ACORNS

1-2-3-4-

A - corns grow on the old Oak Tree —.

ANTS

1-2-3-4-

Ants came amb - ling, one, two three —,

crawled up Al - bert, tick - led his knee —.

Lesson 3

Hold your recorder, balancing the
mouthpiece against your chin.
With your left thumb and first finger,
make the note B.

What must you do to make the note A?

That's right! It's simple. Just add your
second finger and you are playing A.
Remove it, and you are back to B.

Try this several times with your recorder
still on your chin. Then go on to the songs.

Don't forget to SING, CLAP and PLAY.

REMEMBER
IS YOUR **RIGHT** THUMB
IN THE **RIGHT** PLACE?

Sing, Clap and Play 3

At the beginning of every tune are two numbers. These help to tell you the rhythm of the music. Till now there have only been *walking* rhythms:

$\frac{4}{4}$ ♩ ♩ ♩ ♩

left, right, left, right

The new rhythm on this page is a **skipping** rhythm:

$\frac{6}{8}$ ♩ ♪ ♩ ♪

skip and skip and

SKIPPING

Count –
1 and 2 and

Skip and hop, and skip and hop!

DING DONG DELL

1-2-3-4-

Ding! Dong! Dell —! Puss-y's in the well —!

JACK

1 and 2 and

Jack be nim - ble, Jack be quick, Jack jumpov-er the can - dle - stick.

Lesson 4

Look at the picture on the right.
Can you see how to make the note G?
It is made with the thumb and
three fingers of the left hand.

Keep practising G until you get
a clear, round note.

If it squeaks, then you are not
completely covering all the holes.[1]

Always listen to what you play.

[1] Small hands often find
it difficult to reach a G.
Keeping the fingers at
right angles to the recorder
will make the task easier.

G

REMEMBER
LEFT HAND AT
THE TOP

Sing, Clap and Play 4

GILBERT

1-2-3-4-

Gil - bert Gob - lin gob - bled up goats.

This sign ⨟ is called a rest.
It is placed where we want a gap in
the music instead of a note.

HUMPTY DUMPTY

1 and 2 and

Hump - ty Dump - ty sat on a wall —.

FLY AWAY

1-2-3-4

Fly a - way Pe-ter, fly a - way Paul —, Come back Pe - ter, come back Paul —.

11

Lesson 5

So far you have learned the notes B, A and G.

With your recorder resting on your chin,
make the note G. Now lift your third finger.
What note are you playing?
Then lift your second finger.
What are you playing now?

Keeping the recorder on your chin,
practise this several times:

Now play it.

Sing, Clap and Play 5

This sign tells you to repeat the tune.

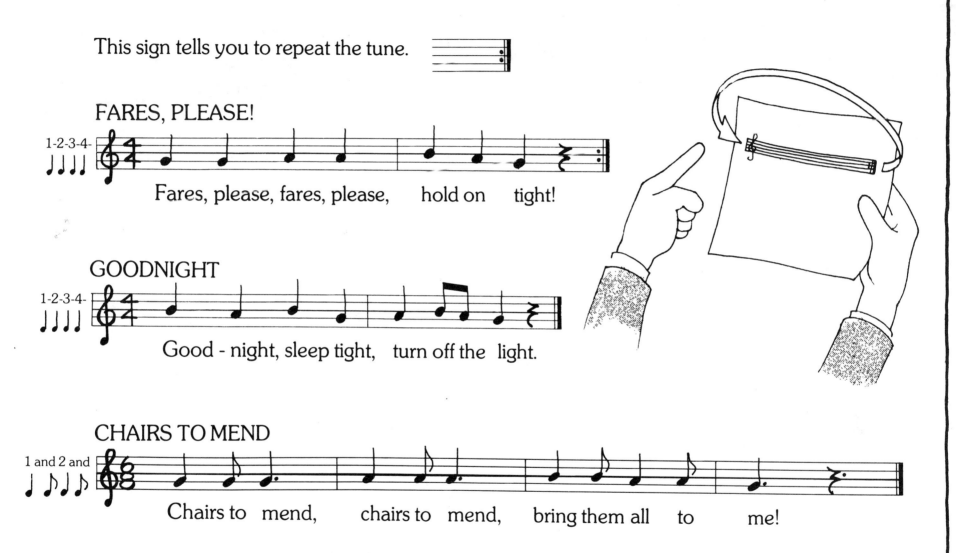

FARES, PLEASE!

1-2-3-4-

Fares, please, fares, please,   hold on   tight!

GOODNIGHT

1-2-3-4-

Good - night, sleep tight,   turn off the light.

CHAIRS TO MEND

1 and 2 and

Chairs to mend,   chairs to mend,   bring them all   to   me!

Lesson 6

Putting notes together can make a tune, but they don't always make good music.

Play this tune, tonguing every note:

(Doo - doo - doo - doo - doo - doo doo —)

Now play the same tune again, tonguing every other note:

(Doo - oo doo - oo doo - oo doo —)

REMEMBER
UNUSED FINGERS CLOSE TO THE HOLES

Joining notes together like this: ♩͜♩ is called *slurring*.

Another way of improving your music is to breathe in the right place.

This is a breathing mark: ✔

Sing, Clap and Play 6

EXERCISE 1

EXERCISE 2

GOODNIGHT

15

Concert 1

AU CLAIR DE LA LUNE

Recorders

1-2-3-4-

Glockenspiel

1 -   2 -   (3 -   4 -)

Recorders

Glockenspiel

Concert 1

ROWING

Slowly

This tune has the same rhythm as 'Jack be Nimble',
but has a slower speed.

Concert 1

CHAIRS TO MEND

 Clapping

1 and 2 and

 Recorders

Clapping

18

Concert 1

FRERE JACQUES

Not too fast

Lesson 7

With your recorder on your chin, make a G.
Now cover the next two holes with the
first two fingers of your RIGHT hand.
This is the note E.

Lift them, and you're back to G.
Keep them close to the holes when
you lift them off.

REMEMBER
LISTEN TO
EVERYTHING
YOU PLAY

Practise changing from G to E,
moving your two right-hand fingers
on and off together.
Now play this:

Sing, Clap and Play 7

ALL ALONE

Slowly

CUCKOO

GIRLS and BOYS

MARCH of the SOLDIERS

This tune fits the words of 'Big Bad Bill'.

Lesson 8

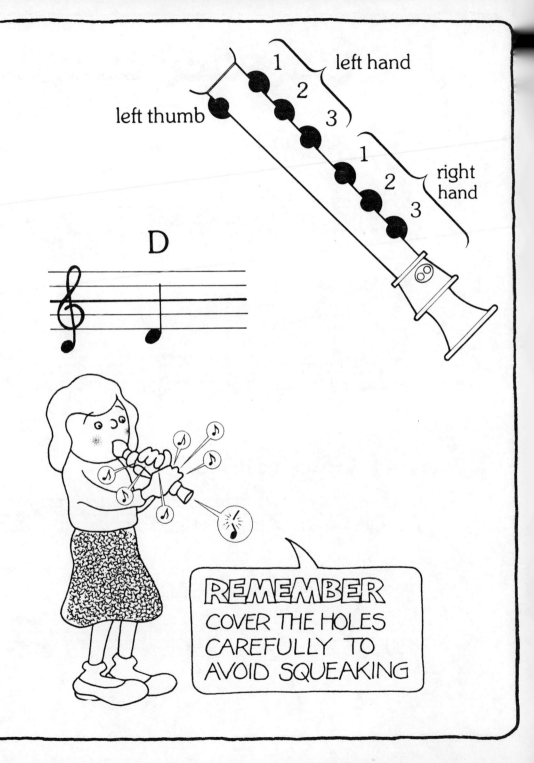

Can you see from the diagram how to make the note *D*?

You use the thumb and three fingers of your **left** hand, and three fingers of your **right** hand.

Play a *D* and keep practising until you get a good, clear sound.

Then play this:

22

Sing, Clap and Play 8

CHINATOWN

1-2-3-4-

A MARCH

1-2-3-4-

SKIPPING

1 and 2 and

ANOTHER MARCH

1-2-3-4-

Concert 2

CUCKOO

Concert 2

A MARCH

Concert 2

CHINATOWN

Concert 2

SKIPPING

All
Recorders
1 and 2 and

Recorders 1

Recorders 2

In the second part of this tune, Recorders 1 start one bar before Recorders 2.

This is called a **round** or **canon**.

You can play this part several times.

Lesson 9

With your left thumb on the back hole,
place your second finger on the second hole.
This is the note C.
Blow it gently.

With the mouthpiece on your chin,
practise moving from C to A.

Now play this:

Next, practise moving from C to B.
Then play this, taking care to make
each note smooth and distinct.

C

left hand

left thumb

2

right hand

REMEMBER
IS YOUR **RIGHT** THUMB
IN THE **RIGHT** PLACE?

Sing, Clap and Play 9

Lesson 10

With your recorder on your chin,
make the note C.
Lift off your **left** thumb,
and you're making *D'*.

Practise this several times.

Now play this exercise, blowing gently.[1]

D' (high D)

left thumb

left hand

right hand

REMEMBER BLOW SOFTLY

[1] Overblowing high notes is a common fault.

30

Sing, Clap and Play 10

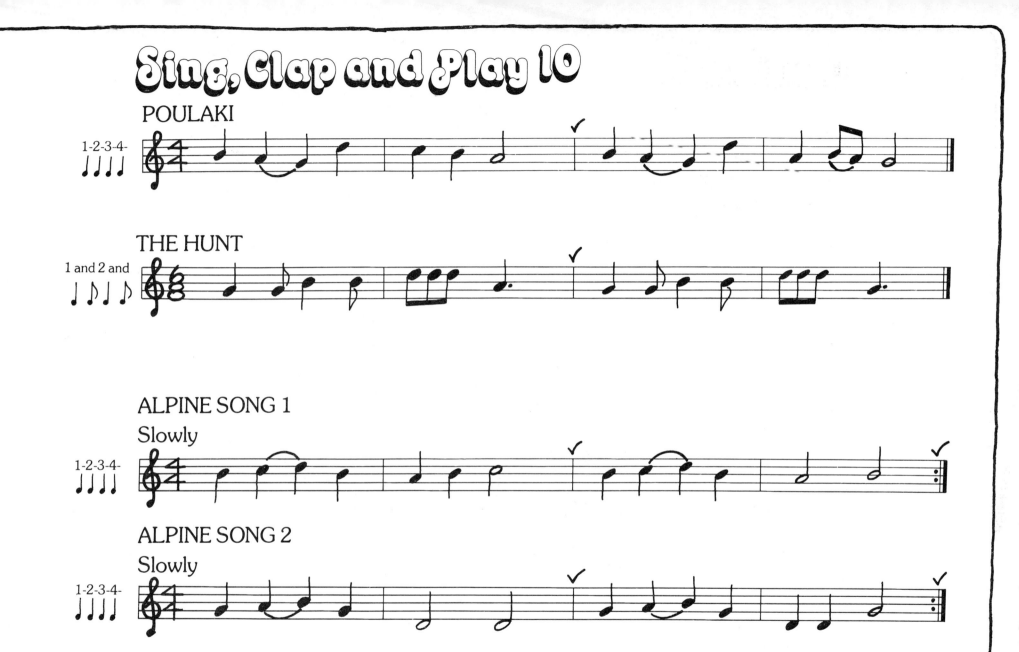

POULAKI

THE HUNT

ALPINE SONG 1

Slowly

ALPINE SONG 2

Slowly

When you have learnt these two Alpine songs,
divide into two groups and play them together.

Lesson 11

This sign # is called a **sharp**.
The new note we are learning
is called **F sharp**, and is written F#.

Play F# and practise it several times.[1]

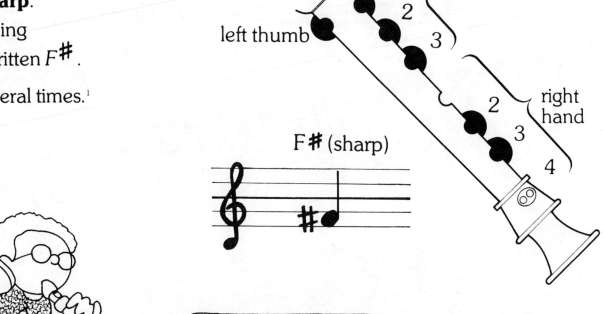

F # (sharp)

left thumb

1 2 3 left hand

2 3 4 right hand

REMEMBER
LISTEN TO
EVERYTHING
YOU PLAY

[1] It is important to check that each finger is on the correct hole, i.e. the first finger is *not* used.

Sing, Clap and Play 11

MARCH 1

MARCH 2

When you have learnt these two Marches,
divide into two groups and play them together.

Concert 3

SUR LE PONT

Concert 3

DAISY, DAISY

Concert 3

MARCH

Concert 3

AMAZING GRACE

Recorders

1-2-

Concert 3

ALPINE SONG

Slowly

Recorders 1

1-2-3-4-

Recorders 2

Recorders 1

Recorders 2

Glockenspiel

Concert 3

ODE TO JOY *L. v. Beethoven*

Not too slowly

Concert 3

ANDANTE *W.A. Mozart*